ESSENTIAL **DK** COMPUTERS

COMPOSING MUSIC
ON YOUR PC

D0524994

ABOUT THIS BOOK

Composing Music On Your PC is an easy-to-follow guide to
creating music on your home computer. This inexpensive
program will show you how to make excellent music.

ODAY'S COMPUTERS MAKE IT POSSIBLE
for anyone to make music at
home. This book will show you
how to do just that. The book features a
program called Dance eJay® 3. In addition
to providing the music-playing software,
the program also includes CD-quality, prerecorded musical phrases, known as
samples. These samples have been created
using real instruments and professional
singers. Whether you're naturally musical
or not, you can use these samples to create
your own original tunes. We'll also show
you how to add your own vocals, apply
special, studio-quality effects, create
accompanying animations, and then save
and distribute finished pieces so that they
can be enjoyed by anyone with a
computer. Making music this way is easy
and quick, and the results will astonish you.

The chapters and the subsections present
the information using step-by-step

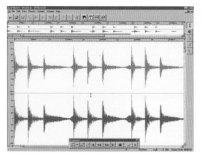

sequences. Almost every step is
accompanied by an illustration showing
how your screen should look at each stage.

The book contains several features
to help you understand both what is
happening and what you need to do.

Command keys, such as ENTER and
CTRL, are shown in these rectangles:
[Enter ←] and [Ctrl], so that there's no
confusion, for example, over whether
you should press that key or type the
letters "ctrl."

Cross-references are shown in the text as
left- or right-hand page icons: ⟮ and ⟯.
The page number and the reference are
shown at the foot of the page.

As well as the step-by-step sections, there
are boxes that explain a feature in detail,
and tip boxes that provide alternative
methods. Finally, at the back, you will find
a glossary of common terms and a
comprehensive index.

ESSENTIAL **DK** COMPUTERS

COMPOSING MUSIC ON YOUR PC

ROB BEATTIE

LONDON, NEW YORK, MUNICH,
MELBOURNE, DELHI

SENIOR EDITOR Jacky Jackson
SENIOR ART EDITOR Sarah Cowley
DTP DESIGNER Julian Dams
PRODUCTION CONTROLLER Michelle Thomas

MANAGING EDITOR Adèle Hayward
MANAGING ART EDITOR Karen Self

Produced for Dorling Kindersley Limited by
Design Revolution Limited, Queens Park Villa,
30 West Drive, Brighton, East Sussex BN2 2GE
EDITORIAL DIRECTOR Ian Whitelaw
SENIOR DESIGNER Andrew Easton
PROJECT EDITOR John Watson
DESIGNER Paul Bowler

First published in Great Britain in 2002
by Dorling Kindersley Limited,
80 Strand, London WC2R 0RL

A Penguin Company

2 4 6 8 10 9 7 5 3 1

Copyright © 2002 Dorling Kindersley Limited
Text copyright © 2002 Dorling Kindersley Limited

Screen shots of Dance eJay® 3 used
by permission from eJay AG

ISBN 0-7513-3708-0

Colour reproduced by Colourscan, Singapore
Printed and bound in Italy by Graphicom

For our complete catalogue visit
www.dk.com

CONTENTS

INSTANT MUSIC-MAKING

PCs are commonly used for processing words, but they're also ideal for making music. This chapter explains how a music program works, and what you'll need to get started.

HOW CAN A COMPUTER MAKE MUSIC?

Everyone is familiar with computers being used to write letters, keep track of the family finances, and play games; but the notion of using them to make music is less well understood, even though it's very straightforward. Just as the contemporary PC has all the hardware needed to write a letter – a keyboard for typing, a screen for displaying the words, and a printer to produce a hard copy – it also has everything you need to make music almost instantly – a sound card and a pair of speakers. With both letter-writing and music-making, all you have to do is buy the software that tells the different parts of the computer what to do.

ANATOMY OF THE SOFTWARE
● Instant music-making software is typically made up of two components.
● The first is a selection of prerecorded chunks of music, called samples, usually organized by instrument and also often by tempo.
● The second is a program with which you can arrange the samples into a piece of music. This is usually instrumental, but sometimes also incorporates vocal samples.

eJay's samples cover almost the whole range of musical sounds, from electric guitar to human voice. It also includes a mixing desk, along with a wide variety of sound-editing and arranging tools.

CHOOSING THE RIGHT SPEAKERS

In the same way that a good stereo system will enhance your enjoyment of a favorite CD, so a decent pair of speakers will help you get the best out of making music on your PC at home. Ideally you should look for a set that combines traditional stereo speakers, which sit on your desk, with a much larger subwoofer, which sits on the floor. This combination will give you a good stereo reproduction, with plenty of bass response.

*ALL IN
THE OUTPUT
Although headphones
are likely to make you
more popular, there's
no substitute for a set
of powerful speakers.*

*CD-Writer
and sound card*

*SPREADING THE SOUND
Although it's easy for other people
who own a copy of Dance eJay to
be given copies of your songs,
writing them to a CD is the one
method that's guaranteed to make
them available to anyone
who'll listen.*

WHAT KIND OF SOUNDS CAN BE PRERECORDED?

Naturally any sound can be recorded and saved as a sample. Collections of samples are usually biased in favor of those who prefer making dance music, but you'll also find vocals, special effects, and all kinds of weird noises alongside the more usual drums, basses, keyboards, guitars, and synthesizers. The big challenge for you is to put them together in a way that sounds good.

TURNING PRERECORDED MUSIC INTO AN ORIGINAL TUNE

Now that you are equipped with a computer that has a sound card and a pair of speakers, and you have a music program and a collection of samples (usually on a CD-ROM), how do you combine these elements to make a piece of music?

PUTTING IT ALL TOGETHER

● First, install the music program onto your computer, then use it to load and organize the samples.

● Most music programs use a window containing a grid of horizontal tracks on which the samples are placed. Vertical indicators show where the bars of music begin and end.

● Individual samples are represented by rectangles, which are dragged onto the grid and snap to the nearest beat. This ensures that your music is always exactly in time. By starting with drums and adding other instruments, a complete song can be built.

● All music programs contain the facility to listen to samples – either individually before you've placed them in your arrangement, or in combination with other samples on the grid.

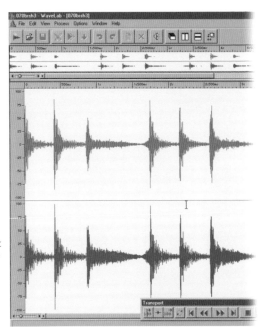

This is what a CD-quality, stereo sound actually looks like when you analyze it with a sound-editing program – the red and blue squiggles represent the left and right stereo channels. There are several such sound-editing programs downloadable from the internet. The program shown here is WaveLab.

SAMPLES BY THE THOUSANDS

You can buy immense libraries of sounds on CD-ROM to use in your own compositions. In the library shown here, Monster Pack 12000, the sounds are arranged according to instrument, tempo, and style. Samples such as these are professionally recorded to the highest quality, so that they can be played back at high volumes without any background noise appearing or unintended distortion.

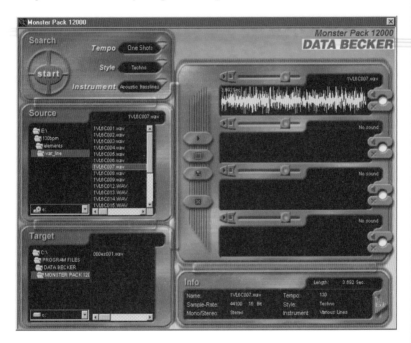

COMPOSING REAL MUSIC

This copying and pasting of samples approach to music-making is different from more conventional methods of computer-based musical composition. The other methods typically involve using a musical keyboard (usually a synthesizer) to create new, original pieces of music, before arranging them into a finished tune or song. With instant music-making, all you need is a library of sample sounds and a program that lets you arrange them in different ways. You don't need to be able to play a musical instrument at all.

INTRODUCING eJAY

Now that we have gone through a little of the theory of making
music with a computer, let's take a look at the music program
that is featured throughout the book – Dance eJay 3.

LEARNING DIFFERENT PROGRAMS

There are a number of music-making
programs and, fortunately, most work in
approximately the same way. When you've
learned how to use one, you'll quickly be
able to pick up another. We have used
Dance eJay 3 in this book as it's one of the
best and well-known programs around.
Let's begin with a quick tour.

MUSIC AS PRESENTED BY eJAY

- As you can see, eJay is a
colorful and lively looking
program. Here, a tune (or
"mix") is ready to be played
by using a set of CD player-
style controls.
- The music is represented
by the colored rectangles
arranged across the grid.
Each one is a sequence of
musical notes or a pattern
of drum beats. These are
just a few of the thousands
of samples included on
eJay's CD-ROM.
- You can arrange these
samples on the screen in
countless thousands of
different ways to produce
unique and original tunes.

INSTALLING DANCE EJAY 3

Before you can use a computer program such as eJay, you need to install it onto your computer. You'll need Windows 95 or above, a 300MHz processor, 32Mb of RAM, 100Mb free hard disk space, 256 colors, a 16-bit sound card, and a CD-ROM drive. Dance eJay 3 can be played through speakers or headphones.

RUNNING THE INSTALLATION

● Put the CD-ROM into the drive. The installation should start automatically.

● There are three install options: **Quick Start**, for people who want to start composing immediately; **Full Installation**, this places more than 600Mb of samples on your hard drive; and **Minimal Installation**, which places some of the samples on your hard drive, and is the installation recommended by eJay.

● The program's files are copied onto the hard drive of your computer. You can monitor this happening via the progress bar.

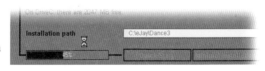

● Once the 100% figure is reached on the bar, eJay asks if you'd like to start the program. Click on **Yes** if you want start immediately.

THE eJAY PLAY WINDOW

Virtually every control is located in the **Play Window** so that you can concentrate on making music rather than moving from window to window. The buttons on the menu bar (**29**–**39**) are explained more fully on the following two pages.

PLAY WINDOW KEY

1 Balance control shifts sample sound left or right.
2 Record prepares a track for recording your sounds.
3 Track number.
4 Solo button to hear sounds on that track only.
5 Mute stops sounds on the track from playing back.
6 The Groove track, where you add your own drum patterns.
7 Current song position as time and bar number.
8 Overall volume.
9 Overall pitch.
10 Drag the slider to move quickly through your song.
11 Turns Booster graphic equalizer on and off.
12 Turns Booster compression on and off.
13 Stereo button to turn the stereo effect on or off.
14 Individual samples are shown as colored blocks.
15 Play controls: Play as Loop; To the Start; Rewind; Stop; Play; Fast Forward; To the End; Start Recording.

WHAT KIND OF MUSIC CAN YOU COMPOSE WITH EJAY?

Although music-making programs come with a wide variety of pre-made sounds, they're usually skewed toward making instrumental dance music. Full-range vocals introduce a level of complexity that isn't easily integrated into a song by the copy and paste methods these programs use. However, the dance category still contains a creative range of styles.

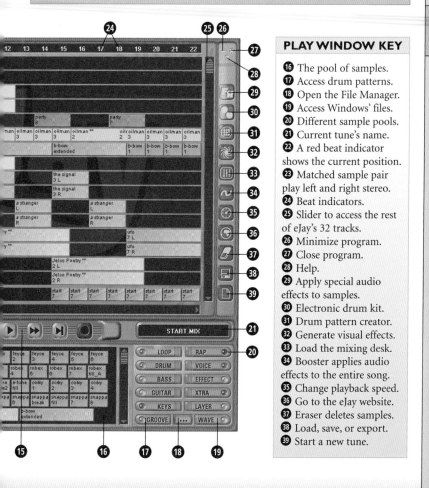

PLAY WINDOW KEY

16 The pool of samples.
17 Access drum patterns.
18 Open the File Manager.
19 Access Windows' files.
20 Different sample pools.
21 Current tune's name.
22 A red beat indicator shows the current position.
23 Matched sample pair play left and right stereo.
24 Beat indicators.
25 Slider to access the rest of eJay's 32 tracks.
26 Minimize program.
27 Close program.
28 Help.
29 Apply special audio effects to samples.
30 Electronic drum kit.
31 Drum pattern creator.
32 Generate visual effects.
33 Load the mixing desk.
34 Booster applies audio effects to the entire song.
35 Change playback speed.
36 Go to the eJay website.
37 Eraser deletes samples.
38 Load, save, or export.
39 Start a new tune.

THE MENU BAR

If you refer back to the illustration on the previous page, you will see that there is a column of buttons down the right-hand side of the eJay window. These buttons are used to control a range of powerful features that will help expand the range and also improve the quality of the songs that you create. Here, we will explain each of the menu buttons in more detail.

MENU BAR BUTTONS

29 **Effect Studio** – clicking the **FX** button opens a new screen containing six audio effects that can be applied to samples. For example, you may want to add "reverb" to your tune to make it sound as if it's being played in a large hall, or tweak its treble and bass using the graphic equalizer (just as you would on a home stereo). You can also edit individual samples to shorten them, fade them in or out, change their pitch, and create harmonies .

30 **Groove Generator** – this is an electronic drum kit that lets you create your own 16-part drum kit from hundreds of different drums. You can also apply special audio effects to each drum.

31 **Drum Matrix** – having created your drum kit, you can then use this feature to construct repeating drum patterns, called loops, which can be incorporated into your music.

32 **Animator** – the **animator** is used to create kaleidoscopic visual effects that represent your tunes in a constantly changing graphic display on your computer screen .

33 **Mixing Desk** – this is where you can control and alter the overall audio picture that you've created. You can change the volume of the samples or their position in the stereo spectrum relative to the other samples .

 The
56 **FX Studio**

 The
45 **Animator**

 The
46 **Mixing Desk**

MENU BAR BUTTONS

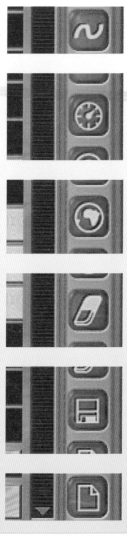

34 **Booster** – this controls three audio effects that can be applied across the entire piece of music (as distinct from the **FX** button, which controls effects that are only applied to individual samples) ⃠.

35 **Adjust Sample Tempo** – music-making programs usually operate at a standard tempo so that the samples play in time. However, if you want to add samples from elsewhere, for example, from sample CD-ROMs or from the internet, they may play at a different speed. With this button, you can alter the tempo to match the one used by your music-making program.

36 **eJay Homepage** – clicking this button launches your web browser, dials your internet connection, and takes you to the eJay homepage. Here, you'll find compositions that have been created with eJay, as well as more samples that you can use, competitions, news, and program updates. It's well worth a visit ⃠.

37 **Eraser** – click on this and your cursor will change from an arrow to a pencil eraser. Use the eraser to delete samples from your tunes quickly. Remember that all you're doing is deleting the sample from the tune – the original sample stays safely either on your computer's hard drive, or on the CD-ROM.

38 **Load/Save** – this allows you to save your mixes onto your computer's hard drive for safekeeping and to load them again if you want to revise them. It's also used to import samples from other sources (for example, the internet), as well as for saving songs and videos – created using the **Animator** – in a format that can be played on other computers ⃠.

39 **New Mix** – this first asks "do you really want to delete your mix?," which only means clearing the current song from the **Play Window**. Clicking on **Yes** means that you can begin creating a new tune from scratch ⃠.

 49 The Booster

 68 The Online Sound Archive

17 Loading a Different Tune

 20 Starting a New Tune

LOADING AND PLAYING A TUNE

Now we're more familiar with the features that instant music-making programs offer, we'll start the eJay program. Although you can begin creating music immediately, it's more instructive to play one of the tunes included on the eJay CD-ROM.

1 STARTING THE PROGRAM

● Click the **Start** button, choose **Programs**, and click on the **Dance eJay 3** option. In the submenu, click on **Dance eJay 3**.

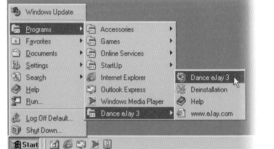

● Ejay loads and, assuming this is the first time you've used it, automatically displays one of the example songs called **Start.mix**.
● The next time you launch eJay, the program will remember the last tune that you were working on and will load that song.

2 PLAYING A TUNE

● Plug in your speakers or headphones.

● Go to the CD playerlike controls in the middle of the screen, and left-click on the **Play** button to play the tune. As the tune plays, the white play bar moves from left to right across the **Play Window**.

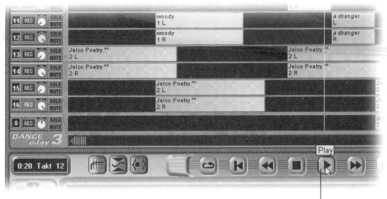

*eJay's **Play** button* ●

3 LOADING A DIFFERENT TUNE

● Now we'll load a different tune. Begin by clicking on the **Load/Save** button in the menu bar on the right-hand side of the **Play Window**.

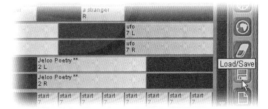

● A pop-up menu appears. eJay refers to completed songs as mixes and gives its files a **.mix** suffix.

● As the current mix is one of eJay's own, there is no need to save it, so simply click on **Load Mix**.

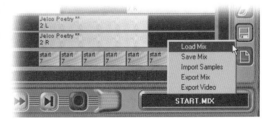

● The **Load Mix** dialog box opens. Look through the list and find a tune that interests you, then left-click on it.

● The title appears in the **File name** text box. Here, the mix **tribalistix** has been selected. To finish loading the mix into eJay, click on the **Open** button.

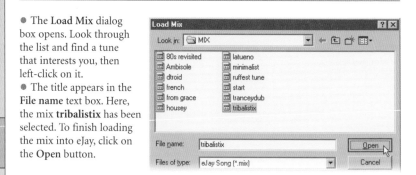

● The samples, represented by the rectangles, are arranged differently in the new tune. Click on the **Play** button to listen to it. You can repeat this process to listen to any of the prerecorded tunes that are included with eJay.

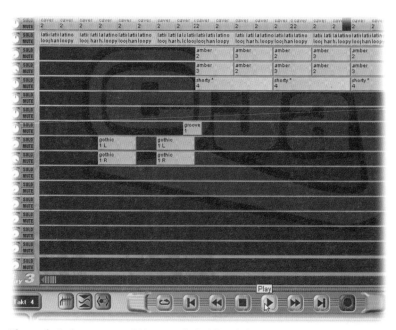

The samples in the new song are laid out completely differently from the first example.

4 CLOSING THE PROGRAM

● When you've finished a session with eJay, left-click on the **Close** button at the top right-hand corner of the **Play Window**.

● As no changes have been made, there's no need to save the mix. Therefore, click on the **Yes** button to quit the program.

PAYING ROYALTIES ON YOUR TUNES

● If you're fortunate enough to make any money out of one of your songs, you may have to pay a proportion of the profits to whoever created the samples in the first place. This applies to all samples, unless they're royalty-free.

● Check the manual and the conditions that come with any samples included with your music-making program, or which are on a CD containing samples, to make sure that they are royalty-free.

USING THE RHYTHM IN YOUR COMPOSITIONS

● One of the reasons that it's very quick and easy to make music with a program such as eJay, is that all the samples are recorded at 140 beats per minute and fit together rhythmically. In this way, you know that a bass part is going to play in time with, for example, the drums and the organ.

● Part of the skill in composing with samples such as this is to use various tricks built into the menu bar to make the music sound less robotic.

COMPOSING

In this chapter, we will show you how you can use the Dance eJay program to create a simple, yet professional-sounding, dance-style piece of music using prerecorded samples.

RECORDING YOUR FIRST TUNE

First, we'll concentrate on the basics of making music, and begin by starting a new tune. To add a sample, you'll listen to (or audition) one and copy the sample by dragging it from the sample pool and positioning it in the **Play Window**. This process is repeated until you've built up a complete tune that can be saved to disk.

1 STARTING A NEW TUNE

● When you launch eJay from the **Start** menu ⌐ it loads the last piece of music you were working on. In this case, the last song was the **tribalistix.mix**.

● This can be overwritten by clicking on the **New Mix** button at the foot of the menu bar ⌐.

┌16┐ **Starting the Program**

┌15┐ **Menu Bar Buttons**
  ❸⁹ New Mix

● An eJay box opens and asks **"Do you really want to delete your mix?"** This is misleading, as clicking on **Yes** only removes the song from the Play Window. You can safely start a new song by clicking on **Yes**.

2 BEGINNING WITH A DRUM TRACK

● It's usually best to start a song with a drum track to provide a rhythm for your composition. When eJay first loads, it automatically opens the pool of **Loop** samples.

● To hear one of the samples, double-click on it with the left mouse button. In this case, a sample named **b-bow 1** is being auditioned.

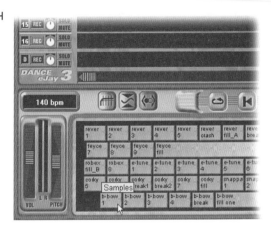

WHAT'S THE DIFFERENCE BETWEEN LOOPS AND DRUMS?

The **Loop** pool contains short passages that are the basis for rhythm in songs and tunes, and are usually played by an entire drum kit. The **Drum** pool contains some loops, but also has hundreds of "one-shots," for example, a single kick on a bass drum or a single hit on a snare, hi-hat, or cymbal. These one-shots can be added to loops to produce color and rhythmic variation.

HOW DO I NAVIGATE THE SAMPLE POOL?

Samples with similar names sound similar – e.g., the **myst1** guitar and the **myst7** guitar. You can sort the samples alphabetically by right-clicking in the sample pool and choose **Sorting: alphabetical** in the menu.

3 ADDING YOUR OWN SAMPLES

● When you've found a sample you like, left-click on it and, holding down the mouse button, drag the sample across the pool.

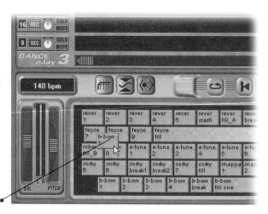

*Dragging a **Loop** sample*

● Continue dragging the sample into the **Play Window** – it's going to be dropped onto the first beat mark of track 1.

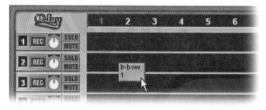

● When you're almost at the top-left corner of the **Play Window**, release the mouse button and the sample snaps into place at the first beat position.

HANDY KEYBOARD SHORTCUTS

Keyboard shortcuts can speed up your music making. (There are Ctrl keys at bottom-left and right of the main keys group on your keyboard.)

Ctrl + O = Load mix
Ctrl + S = Save mix
Ctrl + N = New mix
Ctrl + D = Eraser
Ctrl + Z = Undo
Ctrl + C = Copy samples
Ctrl + V = Paste samples
Ctrl + X = Cut samples

Ctrl + A = Select all samples
Spacebar = Start/stop
← = Rewind
→ = Fast forward
Home = Go to the start
End = Go to the end

4 COPYING A SAMPLE

● You can copy the first sample to make the drum track longer. Remember that sample loops such as this are designed to fit seamlessly together so that you cannot hear the seams.

● With the cursor over the drum sample, right-click on it and, with the right mouse button held down, drag the cursor to the right. A copy of the sample, with a hatched pattern, attaches itself to the mouse cursor.

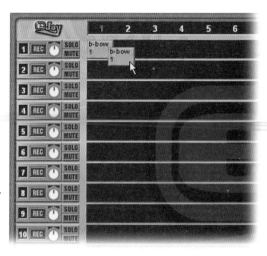

● When the copy is hovering below the next beat mark, release the mouse button and the sample snaps into position.

● Repeat these steps until you have a drum track that is made up of 10 samples. If one of the samples snaps into the wrong position, pick it up by clicking on it with the left mouse button, and while holding down the button drag it to the correct place. At the end you should have a screen that looks like the one below – 10 drum samples in a line on the first track with no gaps.

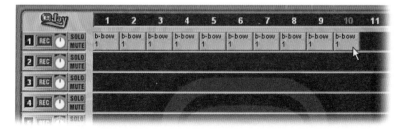

● Click on the **Play** button to listen to the drum sequence.

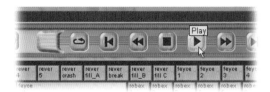

● Click on the **To the Start** button to return to the beginning of the song.

5 ADDING MORE INSTRUMENTS

● Next, add some bass. The different sample pools are listed to the right of the **Play Window**. Click on the **Bass** button and the sample pool changes.

● Double click on different bass sounds to audition them until you find one that you like. Then, click on it with the left mouse button and drag it out of the sample pool and onto the **Play Window**. All samples work in this way.

● Drag the bass sample to the first beat of track 2 and release the mouse button. The sample snaps into position.

● Using the same technique as used earlier, make copies of the bass sample until the bass line lasts the same number of beats as the drums. As before, click on the **Play** button to listen to the drum and bass lines that you've created.

6 NAVIGATING THE SAMPLE POOL

● Up to now, the samples we've chosen have all come from the part of sample pool that you can see when the pool is first opened onscreen. However, this is just a small part of the pool, and there are many more samples. This is where the slider button comes in. First, change to the **Keys** sample pool.

● Next, left-click on the slider to the right of the sample pool and drag it downward. You'll see that the pool scrolls upward through the samples. All the pools work in this way.

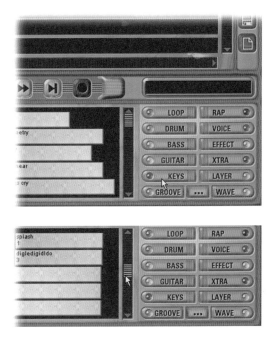

7 ADDING A STEREO SAMPLE

● If you scroll through the **Keys** sample pool as described in the previous step, you'll notice that a number of the samples have identical names, but are differentiated by an **L** or an **R**. These letters show that the samples are a stereo pair, and the letters indicate which channel they will play through.

● Scroll through the **Keys** pool and audition stereo samples until you find one you like. Left-click on the rectangle that's marked with the L channel-letter, and drag and drop the sample between the sixth and seventh beat positions in the **Play Window**.

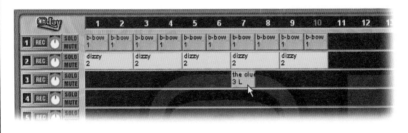

● If we played the combined samples now, they would all play through both speakers. To make sure that the left-channel **Keys** sample only plays through the left channel, move the cursor over the **Stereo Position** control for track 3.

WHERE TO FIND MORE SAMPLES

● You'll find that there is a range of commercially produced sample libraries available to buy on CD-ROM. The creators of Dance eJay 3 sold four different collections at last count. There are also a number of other sites that you can visit on the internet. The eJay website has a good selection, but you could also try **www.samplenet.co.uk/** and **www.analoguesamples.com/**. Remember that samples are usually very large files and may take some time to download to your hard drive.

● Click on the stereo
control at about the
8 o'clock position. The
marker moves to that
position and indicates
that samples positioned on
track 3 will now only play
through the left channel.

● Now, when you click on
the **Play** button, the **Keys**
sample only plays through
the left channel.

● Drag the second of the
stereo sample pair (marked
with an **R**) onto track 4
below its partner, and click
on the stereo control of
track 4 to move the marker
to the 4 o'clock position.

● Play the samples again.
When the play line reaches
the stereo pair, you will
hear the sound in full
stereo breadth.

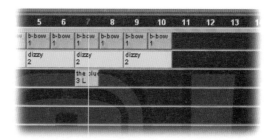

Full stereo is heard at this point ●

8 SIMPLE EDITING

● There are different ways to delete an unwanted sample from your tune, but the easiest works like this. Go to the **Eraser** button on the right-hand side of the screen and click on it. The cursor now becomes an eraser.

● Move the eraser to the sample that you want to erase and click the left mouse button.

● The sample disappears. You can restore it by using eJay's undo command. Hold down the [Ctrl] key on your keyboard and press the **Z** key. To change the cursor back to an arrow, simply click on the eraser button again.

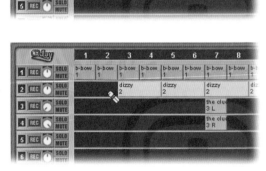

PLAYING ALONG WITH YOUR KEYBOARD

To experiment with the drum sounds, load and play a tune. As the music plays back, tap any of the E, D, C, R, F, or V keys, or the 1 to 10 number keys along the top of the keyboard. The keys will trigger different drum sounds, allowing you to play along with your piece of music.

9 SAVING YOUR SONG

● Let's save the work that has been done. Click on the **Load/Save** button and choose **Save Mix** from the pop-up menu.

● The **Save Mix** dialog box opens, and by default your song will be saved in the **Mix** folder with all the demonstration songs.
● Give the song a name that makes sense to you, such as **My first mix**.

● Click the **Save** button to finish saving your mix to the hard drive.

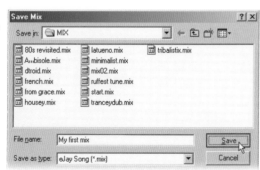

ADVANCED COMPOSING

We'll now show you how to take your compositions to the next level. These tips and tricks will allow you to fine-tune your recordings and make it even easier to create great music.

EDITING YOUR MUSIC

Dance eJay contains many tools and means to edit your tunes. You can have complete control over the volume of a sample, you can change its length for greater effect, and you can position samples with great precision. You can also copy groups of samples that will double the length of your tune almost instantly.

1 COPYING GROUPS OF SAMPLES

● Until now we've been copying samples one at a time, but it's much quicker to copy a number of them simultaneously to build up the rough structure of your tune, and then carry out the editing later. In this section, we're going to double the length of our tune with just a few mouse clicks.

● Load the **My first mix** song and move the cursor into track 5, somewhere near the beginning. Then click and hold down the left mouse button and drag the cursor up. You will see it makes a dotted line.

Dragging the cursor over the tracks

● You'll need to keep holding the mouse button down until you've finished making the copy. If at any time you let go of the button by mistake, simply go back and start again.

● Having dragged the mouse cursor up to track 1, drag it to the right. You'll see a box opening with dotted lines for its borders.

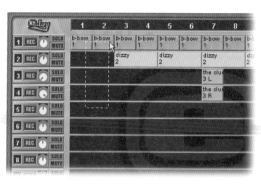

● Keep dragging to the right until you've marked out a rectangle that either covers or touches all of the samples you want to copy. This is important – if a sample is not part of the marked area, it won't be highlighted or copied.

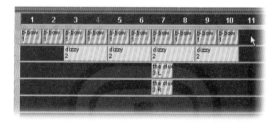

● Release the mouse button and you'll see the dotted lines disappear. You'll also notice that all the samples are now highlighted, indicating that they've been selected and are ready to be used.

● Right-click on the first sample in track 1, and drag the cursor to the right. Although only the first sample appears to move, the rectangle moves with it, indicating that the samples are also being copied.

● As we want to attach these copied samples to the end of the existing section, move the high-lighted are until it is between beats 10 and 11.

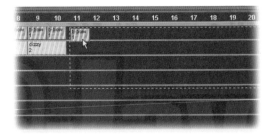

● Release the mouse button – the copies snap into place following the original.
● You now have a piece of music twice as long as the one you began with.

2 CHANGING A SAMPLE'S VOLUME

● Later we'll see how to change the overall volume of a particular track 📄; but before that we want to show you how to change the volume of an individual sample.
● From time to time you may want to change the volume of a particular sample, or pair of stereo samples, in your tune. The easiest way to do that is to edit the sample individually from the **Play Window**.
● Left-click on the lower of the first two stereo

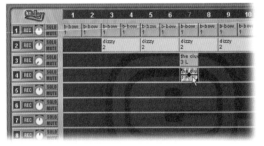

keyboard samples in our musical example.
● Not only is the sample highlighted, you will also see that black lines have appeared at the beginning and end of the

sample, as well as in the middle of it.
● Each of these lines has a small "handle," which you can click on with the cursor and drag to alter the position of the line.

● For now, we're interested in the horizontal line, so click on it with the left mouse button and keep the button held down. A volume control appears.

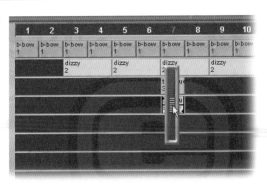

● Still holding down the left mouse button, drag the control down to decrease the volume. Dragging it up increases the volume.

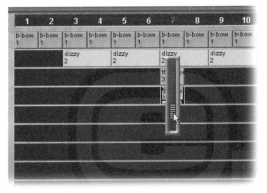

● Release the mouse button and the volume control disappears.
● Take another look at the horizontal line and you will see that it's changed position to reflect the new volume level.
● Repeat the process for the sample above it so that they're at roughly the same level.

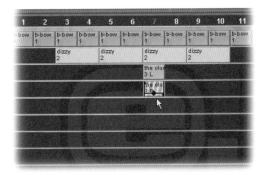

3 CHANGING A SAMPLE'S LENGTH

● As we have already seen, clicking on an individual sample has the effect of displaying black lines at each end. These lines can be used to shorten a sample.

● First, switch to the **Layer** sample pool by clicking on its button.

● Find the sample called **mine1**. This has been chosen because it is a crescendo, which is good to use at the beginning of the tune. It's also long and can be shortened while retaining its effect.

● Click on the sample to select it and drag it into the **Play Window**.

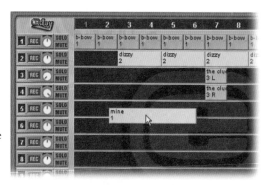

● Place it at the beginning of track 5, release the mouse button, and click on the sample again to select it.

● Move the mouse cursor to the right-hand edge of the sample until it's over the small left-pointing black arrowhead.

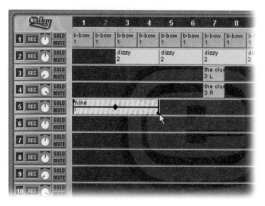

● Click on the arrowhead, hold down mouse button, and drag to the left.

● The outline of the sample remains the same length while the right-hand marker is being dragged across with the cursor. The length of the sample is being shortened.

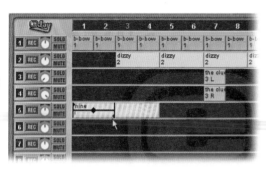

● A good effect can be achieved by stopping the crescendo at precisely the moment the bass starts.

● When the right-hand marker is directly below the beginning of the first bass sample, release the mouse button. You can now play the tune to hear the effect.

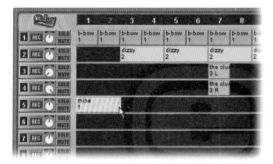

4 PRECISION TIMING

● There are times when it's useful to position the samples more precisely than by using the default "snap" feature. Here, we'll produce a pseudo-choir effect by repeating a vocal sample on different tracks at much smaller intervals – this will sound like there are lots of people singing.

● Click on the **Voice** pool button.

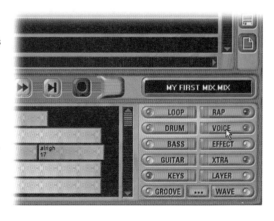

● Next, click and drag one of the vocal samples into the **Play Window** – here, a simple "ahhh" sound has been selected.

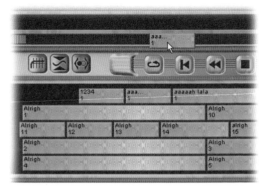

● Drop the sample in the middle of measure 11 on track 6.

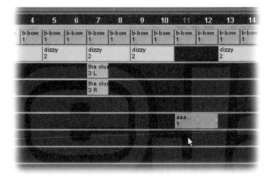

● Now make a copy of the vocal by clicking on it with the right mouse button and dragging it to the track below.

● If we leave things as they are, we'll just have the voices singing in unison. What we want to do is stagger them so that one starts slightly after the other. The small stagger tricks listeners into thinking that there's more than one person singing. However, it is also subtle enough so that it doesn't sound as if the vocalists are singing out of time. The resulting effect is of several people singing along

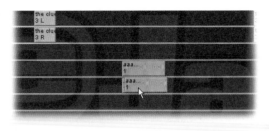

together and disguises the fact that the two samples are identical.

● Hold down the Ctrl key, click on the bottom vocal sample with the left mouse button, hold it down, and drag to the right.

● Using the Ctrl key like this switches off the "snap" feature and, instead, divides the bar into 16ths of a beat.

● Watch the indicator just above the main volume control at the bottom left of the screen. This normally displays the current song position in measures, minutes, and seconds.

● As you hold down the Ctrl key and begin to drag the vocal sample, it changes and displays the current position of the sample in the bar in 16ths of a beat.

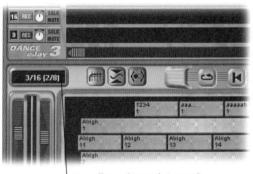

• *Beat offset as the sample is moved*

● When you've moved the sample along slightly, release the mouse button.

● Make as many copies as you want, drop them onto a different track, and slide them along to create the staggered effect.

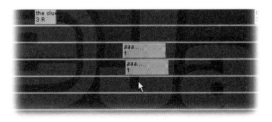

ARRANGEMENT TRICKS

❶ At the beginning of a song, try completely leaving out either the bass or drum part for a few beats. It's very effective when the second part kicks in.

❷ Although it can sound odd on a conventional piece of music, the "dead stop," where everything comes to a complete halt with no sustain from any of the instruments, is very useful in dance music. It helps keep up the interest and the tension in the music.

❸ These vocals have been "layered," as described in the previous section, to give the illusion that more than more person is singing. You can try it with other instruments, and introduce variations – see **⓬** at right.

❹ Because so much dance music is repetitive and perfectly in time, it's easy for it to end up sounding dull and mechanical. One of the ways to avoid this is to completely take out the rhythmic parts (for example, the bass and drum loops) for a few beats. It gives everyone a breather and makes the song sound less robotic.

❺ This keyboard part is only half of a stereo pair and would normally be used along with its partner. However, we've used it here because everything else that is playing at this point is in the center of the stereo mix, and to have a little of keyboard coming out of one channel works very well.

❻ This is a small question-and-answer passage. The **moody** keyboard part starts off by playing a short figure of notes (usually called a riff) and is answered by the lo-fi guitar part. For variation,

we then repeated the short stereo keyboard part used earlier in the tune, then answered it again with the same lo-fi guitar. A question-and-answer section like this contributes to the effect that real musicians are playing.

❼ At this point we've changed the bass and drum parts at the same time to show we've moved into a different part of the tune. Remember that, as all eJay samples are recorded at 140 beats per minute, it doesn't matter if you switch

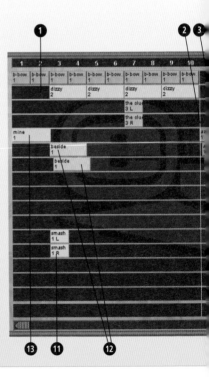

ARRANGEMENT TRICKS

drum and bass samples like this because everything will still be in perfect time.

8 Here, we've used a fast stereo snare drum roll to lead us into the change of bass and drum part mentioned in **7**. This gives a feeling of crescendo and builds excitement.

9 Elsewhere, we've worked hard to limit the number of different instruments and samples being used as this helps to give the tune a style. Rules, though, are made to be broken, and occasionally it's great to use a really different instrument or sample sound. Here we are repeating a single blast on a trumpet.

10 After the silence in the middle section, where we took the drums and bass out and let the vocals carry the tune, it's good to have a couple of smart crashes on the cymbals to bring the rhythm section back in with a bang. We've also repeated the cymbal crashes a few measures later on to help drive the tune along.

11 Just as we've used cymbals to emphasize the returning bass and drums later on, here we've used a stereo sound from the **Effects** pool. It has a percussive sound that serves to emphasize the beginning of a new section – in this case, where the bass enters the tune – but the fact that it isn't a drum sound adds variation.

12 Here, we've staggered a guitar part to provide a variation on the question-and-answer passages described in **6**. The guitar part has been copied and then the copy moved slightly behind the original. Finally, (though you can't see it on the illustration screen) we've decreased the volume. The result is that the guitar part plays with an echo. This can be achieved by using a different method, which is described later □.

13 Another common arrangement trick is to introduce a sample at the beginning that starts quietly and then swells slowly, only stopping when the next chunk of music comes in. Here, the crescendo ends when the bass begins.

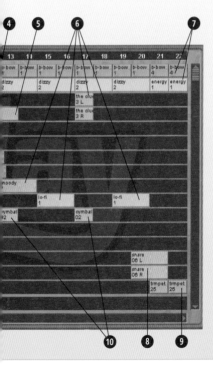

□ Applying Effects 58

ADDING LIVE RECORDINGS

One of the best ways to make your tunes distinctive is to add a unique ingredient – something that you have recorded

yourself. With a microphone plugged in to your sound card, you can sing or rap along with your mix of samples.

1 MAKING THE RECORDING

● First, find an empty track and then left-click on the **Rec** (for record) button. We're recording onto track 16 in order to keep all of the tracks visible in our illustrations, but usually it's best to choose a completely empty track.

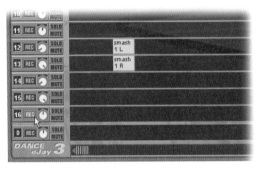

● Make sure you have rewound the song back to the beginning and click the **Start Recording** button in the master control panel,

which is just above the sample pool.
● The tune starts to play back. eJay paints a red rectangle along the selected

track to indicate that your sounds are being recorded. If nothing is being recorded, see later in this book 🗋.

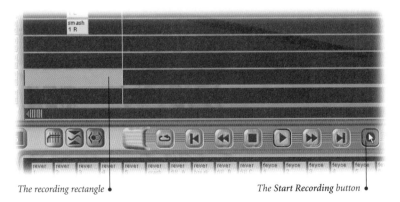

The recording rectangle ●

The Start Recording button ●

🗋 45 **Why Can't I Record Anything?**

● When you've finished
recording, click on the
Stop button. The program
converts the unnamed red
rectangle into a named,
gray sample.

Click on the Stop button to end the recording ●

● To find out where eJay
keeps the recorded samples,
click on the **Wave** button
at the bottom right-hand
corner of the screen.

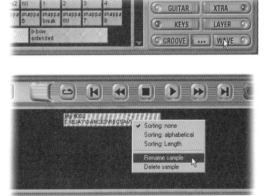

● You'll now see your
newly recorded sound
in the pool.
● To give it a more
meaningful name, right-
click on it and choose
Rename sample from
the pop-up menu.

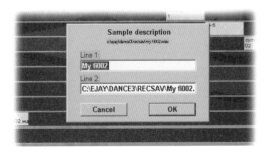

● A dialog box opens in
the center of the screen
with the default name
already in place in the
Line 1 text box.
● Highlight the name by
clicking and dragging the
cursor across it.

● With the text still highlighted, type in a name that is meaningful to you.

● Here, **my vocals** has been chosen. Once you've entered the name, click on the **OK** button to close the dialog box.

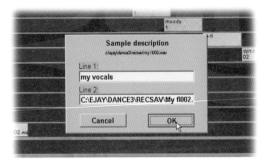

● Your sample is renamed. The second line of text on the recorded sample shows you where the sample recording has been stored on your hard disk.

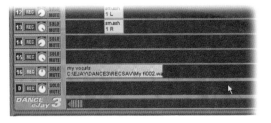

DISTRIBUTING YOUR RECORDINGS

If friends have copies of eJay, you will be able to give them the small mix files that the program uses to store tunes. You can put these files on a floppy disk or email them as attachments. If you want to send your music to someone who doesn't have eJay, save your tunes in a format that can be played back on any Windows computer.

1 EXPORTING YOUR RECORDING

● Click on the **Load/Save** button, and choose **Export Mix** from the pop-up menu.

● To find the exported
tune file easily, we want
to save it onto the
Windows desktop.

● The tune is being saved
in the wav digitized audio
file format. This format
stores sounds as waveforms
and uses **.wav** as the
filename extension.

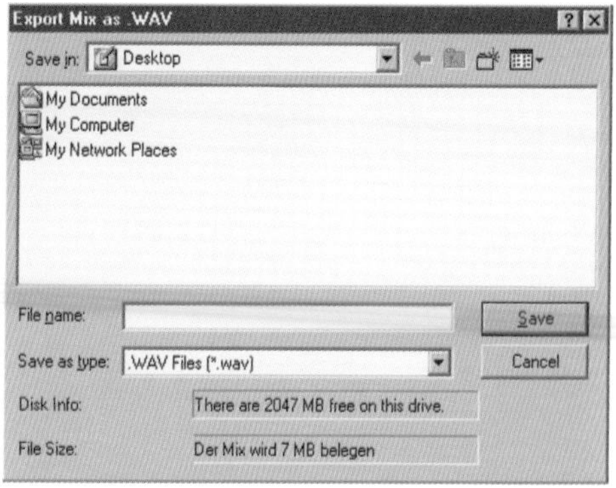

● If you need to navigate
to the desktop, click the
downward pointing arrow
toward the top of the dialog
box and select **Desktop** by
clicking on it.

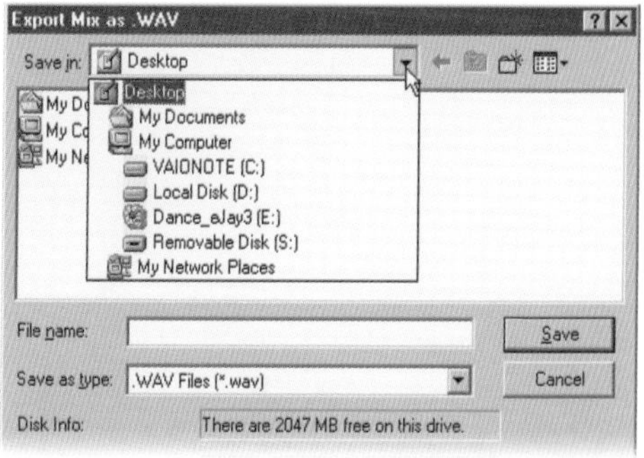

● Type in a name for
your tune, and click on
the **Save** button.

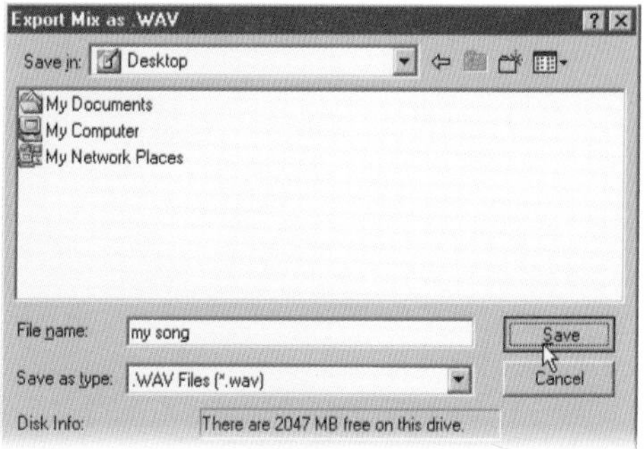

● The program tells you that your tune has been exported successfully.

● Click the **OK** button.

● Minimize eJay by clicking the minimize button at the top-right of the screen, and then find the **my song** (or your own file name) icon on the desktop.

● Double-click on the desktop icon.

● Because the tune has been saved as a Windows wav file, Windows Media Player, which is included with Windows ME, loads automatically and begins playing the tune.

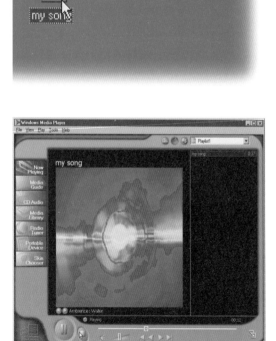

WHY ARE EJAY FILES SO SMALL?

The actual samples themselves are rather large, but eJay's tune files are tiny. This is because they only contain the instructions that tell the program which sound to play, how loud it should be, and where in the stereo mix it appears. Think of it like this – while you could carry the music for Handel's Messiah around in your briefcase, you wouldn't be able to carry the entire orchestra and all their instruments. The advantage of such small file sizes is that you can fit dozens and dozens of mixes on a single floppy disk or send them quickly over the internet. As long as the people receiving the files also have a copy of eJay, they can listen to your music.

WHY CAN'T I RECORD ANYTHING?

Assuming that you've plugged a microphone into the **mic in** connector on your computer's sound card (consult the manual for which connector is which) and that your speakers are connected and turned up, then it's probably because Windows doesn't know what you're trying to record. You can fix this by finding the small speaker icon toward the bottom right of your screen and double-clicking on it. When the dialog box appears, go to the **Options** menu and choose **Properties**. When the next dialog box appears, click the empty circle next to **Recording**, then find the list in the middle of the box and make sure there's a checkmark next to the **Microphone** option. Click on **OK** to close and then click the x button to close the **Recording Control** window. You will now be able to record.

USING THE ANIMATOR

Try clicking on the **Animator** button on the main screen – it looks like a spiral and can be found in the column of function buttons down the right-hand side of the screen. Try playing your song back and watch the TV-style screen in the middle of the **Animator** as eJay goes through its selection of special visual effects that swirl and change color in time to the music. You can either let eJay do the work for you by clicking the **Automode** button, or click on any of the options in the **Wave**, **Color**, **Effects**, and **Pictures** control panels to change the style and movement of the animations. You don't have to use the mouse either. If you look carefully, you'll find a letter or number next to each option, and pressing the relevant key will effect the change.

MIXING

Professional recording studios have a mixing desk for making fine volume and balance adjustments to compositions, and for tweaking the overall sound. EJay also has such a mixing desk.

HOW TO USE THE MIXING DESK

A mixing desk is basically a set of controls for each track in your piece of music. These controls deal with the volume, where the track "sits" in the stereo mix, as well as other elements, such as treble and bass, and one or two extra special effects.

1 LOADING THE MIXING DESK

● Load eJay as usual. If you have followed the earlier example exactly, the piece of music that has been created will load with the program. If you haven't followed the example, don't worry because the mixing desk and the main effects will work in the same way with any tune.

● eJay calls its mixing facility the "mixer," and it can be loaded by clicking on the **Mixing Desk** button.

*The **Mixing Desk** button ●*

• The mixing desk will replace the sample pool at the foot of the screen. Essentially, the same set of controls is repeated 32 times – one set of controls for each of eJay's 32 tracks.

• Although only 16 tracks have been used for the tune that has been created, you can use the scroll bar at the side of the **Play Window** to reveal the remaining empty 16 tracks.

2 USING THE SOLO BUTTON

• We'll begin by using the **Solo** button, which allows you to listen to a single track. Click on the **Play** button to start the tune. Then click the **Solo** button at the foot of the volume fader of track 1, which contains the drum samples. After a beat or two, the other tracks stop playing and you'll hear the drums on their own.

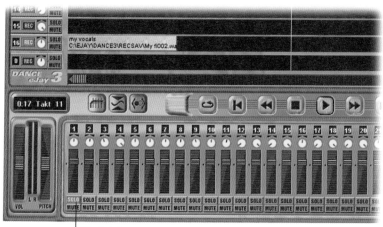

• *The Solo button*

3 USING THE MUTE BUTTON

● Now try using the **Mute** button. With the tune playing, click the **Mute** button at the foot of track 1. This time, you will hear every sample playing except the drums.

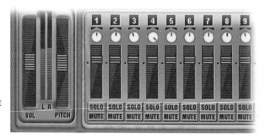

4 USING THE VOLUME SLIDERS

● As you can see, eJay sets every sample to the same volume; but, depending on the different elements in your composition, you may wish to change the settings. For example, the trumpet on track 16 may be too loud and dominant.
● Left-click on the volume slider on track 16 and, still holding down the mouse button, drag the slider down to decrease the volume of this track.
● The volume of any of the tracks can be controlled in this way, including recorded tracks.

5 THE BALANCE CONTROL

● Change the balance of the guitar on track 10 so that it plays more out of the right channel. To do this, place the cursor over the stereo control.

● Still holding the left mouse button down, drag the line around to the right. You'll see the knob appear to move, and the line now points toward the 4 o'clock position. You can make these adjustments to any of the 32 tracks.

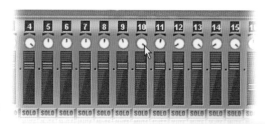

USING THE BOOSTER

The **Booster** is a selection of effects and tone adjustment controls that are applied to the entire tune. In some cases, the samples have been so well recorded and balanced that you'll only need to make minimal adjustments at this stage. In others, however, you might need to increase the treble by a certain amount, emphasize the bass, or make the overall composition sound a bit louder without distorting the samples. The **Booster** can help you make all these changes.

1 LOADING THE BOOSTER

● Like most of eJay's main features, you load the **Booster** by clicking on its button on the right-hand side of the screen.

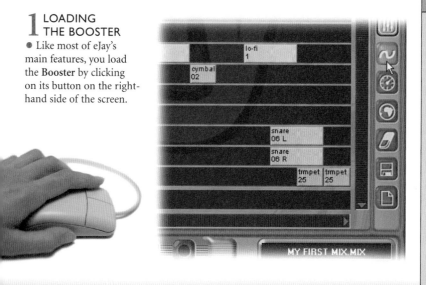

● The **Booster** loads and replaces the sample pool at the foot of the screen, just as the mixer did. You'll see that the **Booster** comprises three distinct sections – **Stereowide**, **Compressor**, and **Equalizer**. These effects can be applied singly to the piece of music, combined in a pair, or all used at the same time.

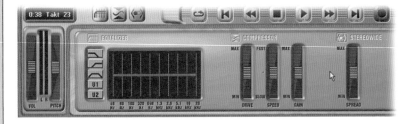

2 USING THE BOOSTER EFFECTS

● Before we can try out any of the effects here, we need to switch them on. Starting with the **Stereowide** effect, click on the Stereo On/Off button to switch on the effect.

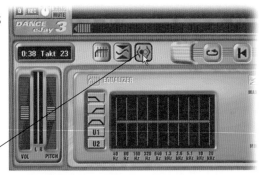

Stereo On/Off button ●

● Rewind the tune to the beginning and click on **Play**. Click on the **Stereowide** slider and drag the slider up. As you do, you will notice that the sound seems to "widen" in each of the channels to produce a broader stereo effect.

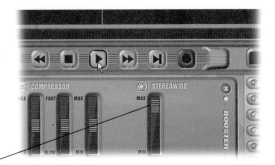

Stereowide slider ●

● Now let's move on and look at the **Compressor**. This is a way of making everything sound louder electronically, but without increasing the volume levels so that they distort. Typically, a compressor makes the loudest sounds quieter so that you can turn the overall volume up.

● It's a little difficult to understand, so the best thing to do is try it out. Click on its button to switch it on.

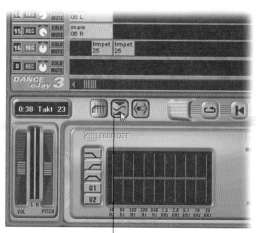

Compressor button ●

● Rewind to the beginning of the tune and click on the **Play** button.

● Click on the **Gain** slider in the **Compressor** and drag it very slightly upward. Listen to the effect as you do this. You should hear the overall volume of the piece of music increasing dramatically.

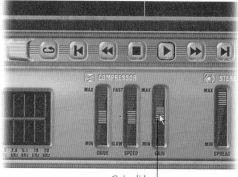

Gain slider ●

USING MIX CONTROLS IN THE PLAY WINDOW

● You will have noticed that some of the mixer controls are also available from the main **Play Window** – the balance, Mute, and **Solo** controls are available down the left-hand side.

● These are useful when composing a tune, but it's still best to use the mixer to produce the final tune because you can then also control the relative volumes of the tracks.

● Leave the **Gain** slider where it is, and now move on to the **Speed** slider. Again, rewind the tune to the beginning and then click **Play**.

● As you listen to the song, experiment with sliding the **Speed** slider up and down – it controls the rate at which the **Compressor** actually kicks in and, again, benefits from very fine adjustment.

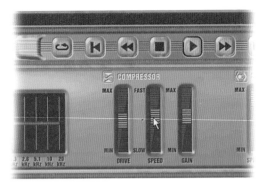

● The **Drive** control looks after the total amount of compression being applied to the tune (this is different from the **Gain**, which looks after volume). Rewind the song, click **Play**, drag the **Drive** slider slowly using the mouse, and listen as you change the setting.

● Getting compression right is a real skill, and the best guides are your own ears. If in doubt, use too little rather than too much.

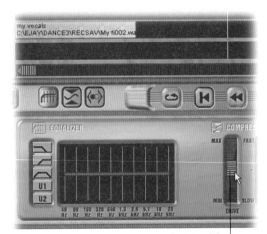

The Drive slider ●

KEEPING THE SAME SOUNDS ON THE SAME TRACK

When putting together the samples for a tune, it's best to keep the same sounds on the same track. This makes it easier to control the volume. For example, if you put an electric guitar and a quiet percussion sound – such as a tambourine – on the same track and set the volume high enough to hear the tambourine, the guitar may distort. Alternatively, reducing the volume of the guitar so it sounds right may render the tambourine inaudible.

3 USING THE EQUALIZER

● After the complexities of the **Compressor**, the **Equalizer** is much more straightforward – it works just like the one on your stereo. Click the **Equalizer** button to switch it on.

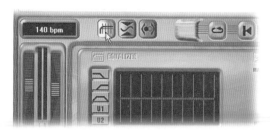

● To the left of the graph window, there are five buttons – three presets and two empty ones labeled **U1** and **U2** where you can store your own settings.
● Click the **Play** button and, as the song plays back, click the first button, called **Low Pass**, on the **Equalizer**. This setting makes the song boomier and more bassy.

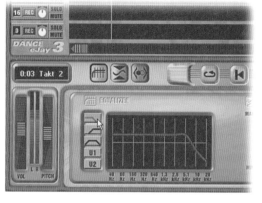

● Now do the same with the second button, called **High Pass**, by clicking on it.

Note how the graphic pattern in the **Equalizer** changes shape. This makes

the tune sound tinnier, as if it were coming out of a small transistor radio.

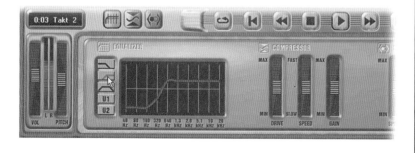

● Try the next preset by clicking on the third button, called **Band Pass**. Again, this drops the bass volume, but adds a distance to the sound as if you were listening to music being played in another room.

● Finally, let's do some of our own tweaking. Click on the **U1** button. You'll see that there's a flat line in the **Equalizer**, indicating that everything's set to the center of the range.

● Rewind the tune to the start and then click on the **Play** button. Move the cursor toward the right-hand end of the line and click on it. Then, still holding down the button, start to drag the line up. It moves like a rubber band.

● Keep listening to the tune and keep dragging the line up. You'll be able to hear how it changes the overall sound.

● Experiment by dragging the line all the way down and see how that changes the sound. You can drag the line back to the center, click elsewhere on the line, drag from there, switch to one of the other settings, or simply switch the **Equalizer** off. The next time you save your tune, all the mixer and **Booster** settings will be saved along with it.

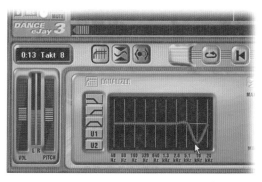

USING THE LOOP BUTTON

● When you're mixing, it can be irritating to keep rewinding your piece of music to the beginning and then clicking on the **Play** button.

● If you're happy to have the song playing the whole time, use the **Play as loop** button (it's to the left of the **To the Start** button). When you click on this button, your song will play continuously.

● When the play line gets to the end of the tune, it immediately returns and starts playing again.

KEEPING ADJUSTMENTS TO THE MINIMUM

● These samples have been carefully recorded to sound really good without too much alteration and amending from you. If in any doubt, make only minor adjustments to the tone, stereo position, and compression of the sample.

● As you become more experienced, you will start to understand what does work and, just as importantly, what doesn't.

SPECIAL EFFECTS

You may need to edit or enhance off-the-shelf music samples from time to time. This chapter shows you how to create unique variations by editing and applying effects to samples.

HOW TO USE THE FX STUDIO

The FX Studio is composed of a selection of special audio effects that can be applied to individual samples. It even contains the tools with which you can edit the actual sounds so that, for example, you can make them fade in and out, become louder or softer, or play them back in a different key.

1 INTRODUCING THE FX STUDIO

● Load eJay as usual and click on the **FX** button ⬜.

● This is the **FX Studio** screen. You can still see the sample pool at the bottom, but the **Play Window** is replaced by an editing window (at the top left and currently empty) and six main effects.

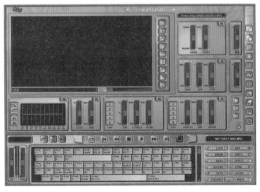

㉙ Effect Studio

• To show you how some of these effects work, we will load a trumpet sample.
• Click on the **Xtra** sample pool.

• If you want to follow the example shown exactly, scroll through the sample pool until you find the **trumpet 25** sample.

Drag it into the editing window in the same way that you drag a sample into the **Play Window**. Alternatively, you can use

any other sample from any pool, as the editing techniques that are going to be used here will work with any sample.

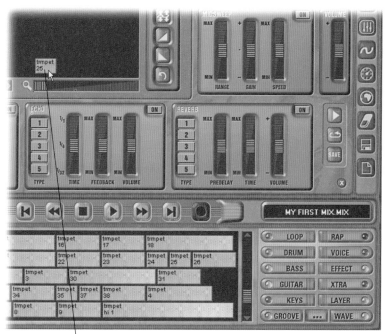

• *The sample is dragged into the FX Studio window*

● When you have dragged the sample into the editing window, release the mouse button. The rectangle is replaced by a visual representation of the sound, in what is known as a waveform. The height of the spikes above and below the horizontal orange line indicates the variations in the volume levels along the length of the sample. Where the orange line has no wave above or below it, it indicates silence.

● Click on the **Play** button to play the sample back. If you've followed this example, you'll hear three short blasts on a trumpet, which correspond to the three surges in the waveform's shape.

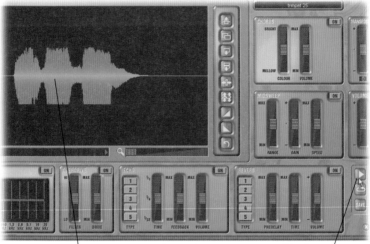

● *The central surge in the waveform*

Play button ●

2 APPLYING EFFECTS

● Now add some reverb. Reverb simulates the different effects that small or large spaces have on a sound – it's a little like an echo, but more subtle. Click the **On** button in the **Reverb** effect panel.

The Reverb On button ●

● There are five presets down the left-hand side of the **Reverb** effect panel, each having different levels that simulate spaces of different sizes. Click on the fourth one, and then click the **Play** button again to hear what it sounds like.

● You can apply more than one effect at a time to any sample, so now let's add some genuine echoes. Click the **On** button in the **Echo** effect panel and choose one of the five preset echoes. Click the **Play** button to hear what it sounds like.

● You can continue applying effects, switching them on and off, trying different combinations, until you're happy with the sound. To make the change permanent and to create a new, unique sample, you can save it by clicking on the **Save** button.

● The new trumpet sample appears in the pool, next to the original.

● What you've done is to create a copy of the original, edit it, and then save it, so the original sample always stays safe.

3 MAKING HARMONIES

● Now let's use the **Transpose** effect to create a vocal harmony. Click on the **Voice** button to change to the vocal sample pool.

● Next, find the first **aaa** sample and drag it into the editing window.

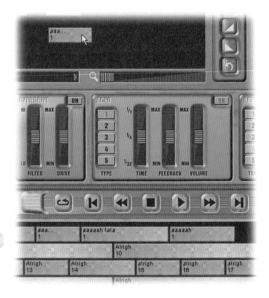

● When you release the mouse button, the new sample replaces the sample that was occupying the editing window – in this case, the trumpet.

● Now move the mouse to the slider that operates the **Transpose** effect.

● Click and drag the slider up three positions, so that the zero at the foot of the slider changes to 3.

● If the **Echo** and **Reverb** effects are still on, turn them off by clicking on their **On/Off** buttons (these toggle between on and off).

● Now click on the **Save** button to save the new vocal sample so that it can be used to create a harmony in the composition.

USING THE CORRECT PLAY BUTTON

When you're using the FX Studio and want to hear how the effects are working, make sure you click the correct **Play** button. If you click the usual **Play** button, you'll start to play whichever song is currently loaded in the main **Play Window**. Instead, make sure you use the FX Studio's own **Play** button, which will only play back the sample that you are currently editing.

● Close the **FX Studio** by clicking on the small **x** at the bottom right-hand corner.

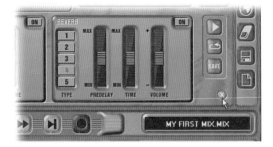

● Back in the **Play Window,** find the new vocal sample in the **Voice** pool. It will be next to the sample that it's based on. Drag it up into the tune.

The new, saved vocal sample ●

CHOOSING THE BEST TIME TO EDIT

There are no hard and fast rules about applying effects, but it's usually best to have the tune mapped out before you start editing individual samples. In this way, you won't get too bogged down in the small details at the beginning. It's preferable to be able to hear the track more or less all the way through, from beginning to end, before starting on any subtle changes.

● As the new vocal sample has been designed to harmonize with the original sample on which it's based, we need to drop it onto one of the tracks so that it lines up with the beginning of the first vocal **aaa** sample on track 5.

● Once it's in position, click the **Play** button and you'll hear that the new sample plays along with the original, but one-third higher. This produces a pleasing harmonic effect, as if two people were singing together.

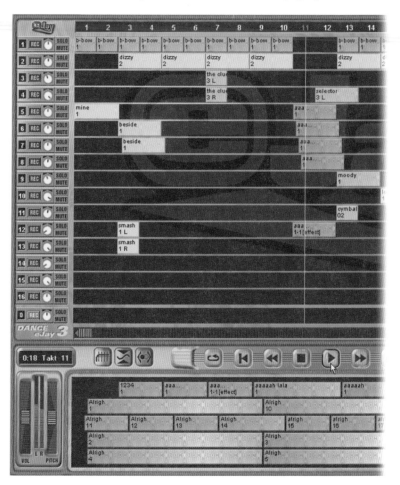

4 EDITING SINGLE SAMPLES

● As well as applying effects to samples, you can actually edit the samples themselves using the editing window and toolbox in the **FX Studio**.

● If you're not already in the **FX Studio**, click the **FX** button.

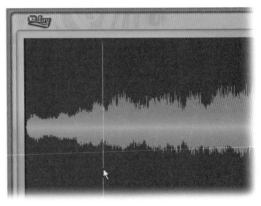

● Although you can work with any sample you want, for simplicity's sake we're going to carry on using the vocal **aaa** sample that's already there. You can see from the waveform that the vocal starts quietly and then gets louder, but we want to make that fade-in even more pronounced.

● Click on the sample, about a quarter of the way in, at the point where it's starting to get louder.

● Still holding down the left mouse button, drag it to the left.

● You'll see that part of the sample is highlighted in blue. This indicates that this section has been selected for editing.

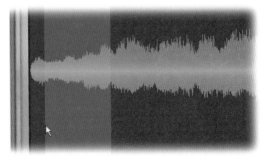

● With the section
highlighted, click on the
Fade In button – it looks
like the lower right half
of a square.

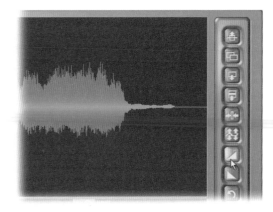

● You can now see that
the shape of the waveform
has been altered. There's
more silence at the
beginning, and it fades
in more gradually.

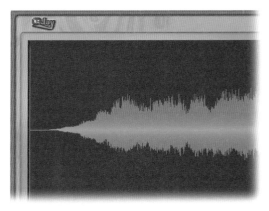

● If you want to undo the
last piece of editing, then
click on the **Undo Last Step**
button. Be aware though,
that it only undoes the last
step and none before.

*The **Undo Last Step** button* ●

● If you want to, you can make a particular part of a sample play back much louder. Start to highlight the area by clicking at the startpoint with the left mouse button.

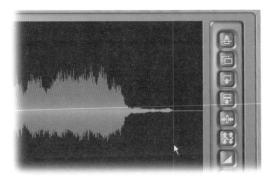

● Holding down the left mouse button, drag to the left to highlight the passage you want to make louder.

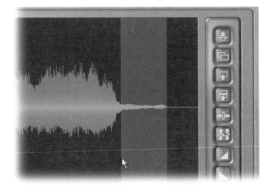

● Then, with the passage highlighted, click the **Maximize Volume** button and watch what happens to the waveform. It expands greatly above and below the central line.

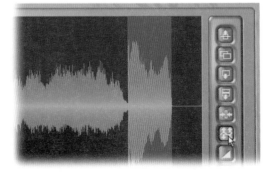

● You can also remove parts of the sample that you don't want.
● Click on the **Undo Last Step** button to remove the volume change, and click near the end of the sample with the left mouse button.

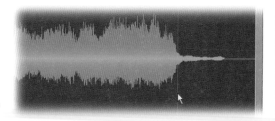

● Drag to the right to highlight the end of the sample.

● To delete the highlighted section of the sample, click the **Cut Selection** button, and that part of the sample is removed.

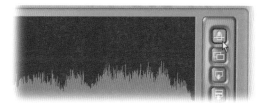

WHAT DO THE EFFECTS DO?

Chorus adds pseudo-harmonies to a sound, making it sound fuller and richer; it's very good for using with guitars. **Midsweep** defines a set of treble and bass settings and then sweeps between them making a sample at first sound open and then closed; it is suitable for synthesized sounds. **Overdrive** makes a sample sound dirtier and more distorted; try it with electric guitars. The **Equalizer** is like a set of bass and treble controls on a stereo; it's especially useful for vocals. **Echo** literally adds a series of echoes; it's good for vocals and sustained sounds, where it makes them sound thicker. **Reverb** changes the space around a recording, tricking the ear into thinking that the sound is being played back in a space from a small club to a large arena; it's particularly effective for vocals.

THE ONLINE SOUND ARCHIVE

You are not limited to the samples supplied on the eJay CD-ROM to develop your special effects. eJay provides access to an online sound archive of samples that have been created by eJay. You can specify the style, tempo, and key that you want.

USING THE ONLINE ARCHIVE

● Click on the web button on the menu bar and select **Online Sound Archive**.

● The **Online Sound Archive** opens in the pool window. Set the **Styles** to **Dance**, the **Tempo** to **140 bpm**, and the **Key** to **A-minor** as these are the settings used in Dance eJay 3. You can then click on **Go!**

● A menu of samples appears, and you can select any one by clicking on it and dragging it into the **Play Window**.
● Now you can listen to the sample, select it, include it in your collection of samples, and add it to your composition.
● Click on any button to return to one of the other eJay screen displays.

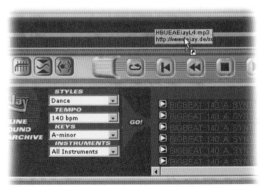

SHARING YOUR MUSIC

● Once you've spent time creating a piece of music, it's the most natural thing in the world to want others to enjoy it too. This doesn't necessarily mean you're going to make any money out of it – aspiring musicians outnumber the professionals many times over. However, there are a number of ways in which you can share your compositions – from making your own CDs to distributing your music on the internet. Here are a few ideas.

● **Floppy disk** – eJay's mix files are very small, and you can comfortably fit an album of music onto a floppy disk to give to friends. Remember, though, that they'll need to have Dance eJay 3 to listen to the music.

● **Wav files** – You can also export your music as a Windows Wav file, which anyone can listen to it on their computer using Windows Media Player. Wav files are large, so you'll need to use a removable disk, such as a zip disk, to handle them. Windows Wav files are much too large to send over the internet as part of an email message. Nor will they be accepted by any of the websites that specialize in promoting music from unknown musicians.

● **MP3 files** – MP3 is currently the preferred format for very new music. MP3 is a way of saving digital songs that play back at nearly CD quality, but which only take up a fraction of the space of a Wav file. This makes them much faster to download using a modem. So, if you export your song from eJay as a Wav file, you can then use a free program, such as MusicMatch Jukebox (available from **www.musicmatch.com**), to convert it into a much smaller MP3 file. For a good source of MP3 sites that accept amateur music, visit **www.mp3.com**. For general related information, try **www.getsigned.com**, which is an excellent site for musicians chasing that elusive first break.

Once your song has been saved as an MP3 file, it can be copied to and played back on any of the digital music players currently available. These are the modern equivalents of the cassette-based personal stereo.

● **CD-ROM** – Perhaps the most convenient way to share your music is to make your own CD-ROMs. This used to be a complex and unpredictable task, but nowadays it's very straightforward. You'll need a home computer with a CD-RW drive, which allows you to record onto special blank CDs. You can buy these from good electrical stores and many music shops. Your CD-RW drive will have software that lets you copy the music you have created using your music program onto the blank CD. You can add track listings, titles, and – with some programs – even CD sleeves and labels.

● **The internet** –Sites exist where you can post your Dance eJay .mix tracks for others to download. One site is **http://fp.keeshnaweb.f9.co.uk/**, which also advertises albums.

GLOSSARY

ARRANGEMENT
Describes the way a group of samples or sounds is assembled to create a song.

AUDITIONING
Listening to a sample before deciding whether or not to include it in your tune.

BALANCE
Sometimes used interchangeably with MIX, it also refers to whether a sound is set to come out of both speakers equally or whether it's directed to play through the left or right channel.

BOOSTER
This control in Dance eJay is for fine-tuning your completed song by means of the equalizer, compressor, and stereo spread.

CRESCENDO
When a song slowly builds in volume to its loudest point, it is reaching a crescendo.

EXPORT
To save a song in a format that can be read and played by programs other than the one used to create it.

GROOVE
Usually refers to a repeating pattern played by the drums and the bass, and which provides the foundations of a piece of music.

LOOP
Any kind of sample that has been recorded so that copies can be attached to it without listeners being able to hear the seams.

MIX
Usually refers to relative volume, balance, and effects applied to all the different instruments in a tune. In the case of the eJay music program, it's also the name of the file type used to store instructions for each tune.

MP3
A way of storing near CD-quality music in a small file. Works by removing the bits of audio information that the human ear is unable to hear.

MUTE
Temporarily prevents the samples on a particular track from being heard when the rest of the tune is being played back.

ONE-SHOT
A single strike of a drum or piece of percussion or a single note of an instrument. Used for emphasis in a piece of music.

PITCH
The degree to which a sound is high or low.

POOL
The repository where samples are stored.

SAMPLE
An individual sound (usually a single instrument) recorded in stereo at 44KHz – that's CD-quality.

SAMPLE LIBRARY
A CD-ROM full of samples divided into instrument types (drums, basses, keyboards, and so on) and played at a different number of beats per minute.

SNAP
An editing feature that makes it easy to line up samples in a tune. When a sample is dragged into the Play window and the mouse button is released, the sample automatically snaps to the nearest predetermined musical position.

SOLO
Temporarily turns off all the other tracks containing samples in a tune other than from the track that is being selected.

TEMPO
The speed at which a sample plays – usually expressed in beats per minute; all Dance eJay's samples play at 140 beats per minute.

TRACK
A row on the Play window grid where samples are dropped. So, for example, you might have the drums on track 1, the bass on track 2, and the other samples spread across the 32 tracks that eJay contains.

UNDO
Cancels the last action that you performed. With eJay, only the latest action can be undone; the program does not undo previous actions.

WAV
The file format employed by Windows for storing digital music at CD quality.

WAVEFORM
A graphic representation of a sound wave that indicates its characteristics.

INDEX

ACKNOWLEDGMENTS

PUBLISHER'S ACKNOWLEDGMENTS
Dorling Kindersley would like to thank the following:
Paul Mattock of APM, Brighton, for commissioned photography.
Redferns Music Picture Library/Fin Costello and
Redferns Music Picture Library/Suzi Gibbons for recording studio images, p.6.
eJay AG for permission to use screenshots from Dance eJay 3.
eJay® is a registered trademark of eJay AG.

Screen shots of Microsoft® Windows used
by permission from Microsoft Corporation.
Microsoft® is a registered trademark of Microsoft Corporation.

Every effort has been made to trace the copyright holders.
The publisher apologizes for any unintentional omissions and would be pleased,
in such cases, to place an acknowledgment in future editions of this book.

All other images © Dorling Kindersley.
For further information see: www.dkimages.com